Tip Tap

Written by Charlotte Raby
Illustrated by Emma Latham

Collins

Tim tip taps.

Sam tip taps.

Dad pats pans.

Tim tips tins.

Dad taps pans.

Sam tip taps.

Sit Tim sit.

Pat Sam pat.

Tim pats. Sam taps.

Dad tip taps.

Pit pat pit pat.

Tap tap tap.

/m/

After reading

Letters and Sounds: Phase 2

Word count: 38

Focus phonemes: /s/ /a/ /t/ /p/ /i/ /n/ /m/ /d/

Curriculum links: Expressive Arts: Exploring and Using Media and Materials

Early learning goals: Understanding: answer "how" and "why" questions about their experiences and in response to stories or events; Reading: children read and understand simple sentences, use phonic knowledge to decode regular words and read them aloud accurately, demonstrate understanding when talking with others about what they have read

Developing fluency

- Your child may enjoy hearing you read the book.
- Encourage your child to read the book again with lots of expression. You may wish to model reading the first two pages, emphasising the "sound" words.

Phonic practice

- Help your child to practise sounding out and blending CVC words.

  S/a/m Sam

  s/i/t sit

  p/a/n/s pans
- Explain that the word **Sam** is a name and so it starts with a capital letter.
- Look at the "I spy sounds" pages (14–15). Say the sound together. How many items can your child spot with the /m/ sound in them? (e.g. *map, moped, mice, music, mural, maracas, mud, mobile*)

Extending vocabulary

- Look at page 6 together. Ask your child if they can think of another word that could be used to describe what Dad is doing, instead of **taps**. (e.g. *bangs, smashes, hits, plays*)
- Now look at page 7 together. Can your child think of another word that could be used instead of **tip taps** to describe what Sam is doing? (e.g. *dances, moves, bangs*)